TOTON DEPOT AND YARDS

PAUL ROBERTSON

AMBERLEY

Front cover: Mainline Freight-liveried No. 58042 *Petrolea* departs from Toton with a loaded MGR, which has been staged on the New Bank for several hours, 7D49 03.21 Thoresby colliery–Willington power station. 12 September 1996.

First published 2022

Amberley Publishing
The Hill, Stroud
Gloucestershire, GL5 4EP

www.amberley-books.com

Copyright © Paul Robertson, 2022

The right of Paul Robertson to be identified as the Author of this work has been asserted in accordance with the Copyrights, Designs and Patents Act 1988.

ISBN 978 1 3981 0398 6 (print)
ISBN 978 1 3981 0399 3 (ebook)

British Library Cataloguing in Publication Data.
A catalogue record for this book is available from the British Library.

Origination by Amberley Publishing.
Printed in the UK.

Introduction

Ask any rail enthusiast or trainspotter through the latter part of the twentieth century where the best place was to observe train movements or obtain numbers, and Toton would be high up on all of their lists. At its busiest, after the Second World War, Toton could boast the largest freight yards in Europe, and third largest in the world, and to this day it remains the depot with the largest loco allocation in the UK.

The introduction of railway yards at Toton came in the mid-1850s, with the need for a location for stabling, sorting and shunting of coal traffic from the rapidly growing Nottinghamshire and Derbyshire coalfields, for use in power generation and industrial use in Leicestershire and the West Midlands.

While hump shunting was the norm at Toton from just after the turn of the century in 1901, modernisation took place with remodelling and mechanised sorting introduced, initially on the Down side from 1939, with the Up side following in 1950/51. In the mid-1950s the Up side was dealing with 3,000–4,000 wagons daily depending on the day of the week, amounting to around a million wagons per year, and at its peak Toton was annually humping over 2 million wagons through its yards.

In the early seventies, modernisation of the actual coal trains that bore the majority of the traffic through Toton (the introduction of the Merry-Go-Round MGR concept) and the closure of many gasworks, with the oncoming availability of North Sea gas, saw wagon throughput slashed. This brought about the closure of the Down hump in 1978, with all remaining wagons requiring humping concentrated on the Up side. This survived a further six years until closure came in 1984, which may have been partly brought about by the miners strike in that year. The yards were subsequently used for Speedlink traffic, stabling/staging of MGR sets and engineering traffic.

The loss of the Speedlink wagonload services in 1991, later followed by the Speedlink coal services, further reduced the requirement for the yards in the early 1990s. By the 2000s, contraction of the Nottinghamshire and Derbyshire coalfields, new bogied, greater capacity wagon fleets, and loss of some traffic to other operators, reduced the requirement for the yards even more. The reductions in traffic, combined with the national financial situation at the time, saw DB Schenker officially close the Up side yards, New Bank and Old Bank, at 23.59 on 26 April 2009. By mid-2010, the financial downturn caused the winding up of operator Jarvis Fastline Freight, and DBS took over operating Daw Mill-Ratcliffe power station services, with Old Bank yard being reopened to stage/run-round these trains. With the burning of fossil fuels being phased out in the UK, and Ratcliffe currently being served by another freight operator, Toton has lost its coal trains once again, but Old Bank remains in use for engineering traffic and the staging of through stone workings. The New Bank, which was mooted at one stage to be reprieved as a base for the Network Rail High Output trains, remains out of use with the connections at the south end now severed. The yard is littered with stored/withdrawn Class 60 locomotives and some rolling stock, but nature had really taken hold with silver birch trees thriving throughout the yard. However, towards the end of 2021, further reuse was suggested when all of the vegetation was cut down, and this also included scrapping of redundant vehicles in the remains of West yard and major tree clearance here too, but as of mid-2022 nothing had progressed. However there are rumours suggesting the Balfour Beatty S&C fabricating site currently located at Beeston, may be looking to relocate to here.

The Down side yard (North yard) has seen some recent investment with the reception lines being fully renewed, and DB Cargo have regenerated the former CM&EE compound between North yard and Meadow sidings, with a car terminal for the import/export of Toyota cars now up and running on this site.

Toton TMD was fully operational early in 1965 and was reputedly the largest diesel depot in Western Europe. With an allocation of between 300 and 400 locomotives during the 1970s/early 80s, and the chance of seeing more than a hundred locos actually on shed, it's easy to see why Toton was so popular. The depot has seen the coming and going of several loco types. Class 20, Peak, Class 56 and Class 58 locos, all synonymous with the depot, have long since disappeared, with the new order of Type 5 Class 60, 66 and 67 being the main types seen on shed these days. Stored Class 60s litter the depot and yards awaiting a reprieve, or more likely scrap (though some have now been sold to DCR). I have been fortunate over the years in being able to visit the depot on many occasions on behalf of various publications to capture newsworthy events, helped by my locality to the complex, having lived nearby since the early 1990s. Prior to those official visits, I used to accompany my father, who, as a local scrap merchant, would often visit Toton to view items of scrap before tendering an offer.

Will HS2 happen? Current plans have seen the Erewash Valley route removed from the proposed Birmingham-Leeds route, with the new railway now only being built as far north as East Midlands Parkway station, and then HS2 trains would use the existing route between there and Nottingham, Derby and Chesterfield. Toton was originally planned for a major transformation with the plans showing all infrastructure on the east side of the main line (Up side yards) swept away to make room for an interchange station and facilities. Therefore with the cancellation of HS2 running through Toton, as suggested above there is now a chance of New Bank and the former West yard being regenerated for a freight railway purpose.

I would like to thank the photographers who have kindly contributed images to help illustrate this publication and fill the gaps in my own collection and pass thanks to my family for having to cope with my railway obsession!

Paul Robertson
www.Toton-Rail.co.uk
May 2022

The typical view seen during the 1970s and 1980s as you entered the main entrance to Toton depot from Station Road, Stapleford. (P. Kazmierczak)

An additional string to my photography bow was added in 2020 when I decided to buy a drone. This has allowed me to photograph Toton from totally new viewpoints and angles, showing what a vast railway location this still is, even with the loss to nature of some of the former yards. In this view, there are six different liveried Class 66s on view, four of which are on one train. No. 66587 *AS ONE, WE CAN*, leads Nos 66554, 66044 and 66051 *Maritime Intermodal Four* away from Toton with 6K50 15.13 to Crewe Basford Hall, passing GBRf No. 66713 *GM Forest City* and another Freightliner 66 in North yard. 21 September 2020.

For many, a trip to Toton would involve a walk from Long Eaton station, or maybe a Barton bus ride from Nottingham or Derby to Long Eaton Green, so the first view of the railway and, if you were lucky, a train may have been around the road bridge over the line in the town. Here looking south from the bridge No. 56095 is seen approaching with the lightly loaded 6D36 05.49 Bescot yard–Toton yard. 13 June 2003.

From the other side of the road, looking north, 6K50 15.13 Toton yard–Crewe Basford Hall yard is approaching headed by three different classes of loco. EWS-liveried No. 60022 leads Wrexham & Shropshire-liveried No. 67012 *A Shropshire Lad* and EWS-liveried No. 66176. 25 August 2009.

English Electric Type 1s Nos 20194 and 20063 depart from Toton with an unfitted loaded coal working, heading towards Trent East junction and possibly for Castle Donington power station. Vegetation and the sighting of new colour light signals prevent an exact same angle being obtained in the present day. 28 April 1978. (J. Woolley)

Taken from the nearest possible angle to compare to the previous image, which was taken forty-four years prior, Colas Rail Freight-operated No. 56302 *PECO The Railway Modeller 2016 70 years* departs from Toton with 6K35 09.23 Stapleford and Sandiacre sidings–Longport Pinnox sidings with used ballast for recycling. A new signal prevents going any wider to the right now. 22 February 2022.

Taken from the overflow car park to the rear of the Long Eaton Asda store, Mainline Freight-liveried No. 37798 arrives at Toton with 7B11 13.18 Derby station–Stapleford and Sandiacre yard. The semaphore signal was a legacy left over from when Long Eaton oil terminal was in use, the signal lingering on until signalling renewals took place in 2008, even though the terminal was closed by the mid-1990s. 28 July 2002.

Seen from atop the high-level flyover, disused and devoid of track at this time, No. 60065 *Kinder Low* approaches on the Down main line with 7A23 16.55 Nadins DP–Toton New Bank MGR, with coal for later tripping to Ratcliffe power station. 4 June 1997.

Mainline Blue-liveried No. 58023 *Peterborough Depot* arrives on the Down goods with MGR empties running as 6P45 08.45 from Drakelow power station. 25 May 1999.

The high-level bridge has long since hosted its last freight trains passing over, but still remains in place over the Erewash main line and is now likely to survive indefinitely with HS2 plans now abandoned on this route. During 2008 part of the parapet wall fell down allowing this view of No. 66105 approaching with 6D44 11.32 Bescot Yard–Toton Yard. 24 October 2008.

Class 56s meet at Toton East Junction with No. 56052 departing with a loaded train for Ratcliffe as No. 56071 arrives with a set of empties from the power station. 5 April 1982. (P. Robertson Collection)

Grimy No. 58046 *Asfordby Mine* ascends the Up high-level goods from Toton Junction working 6F71 13:46 Toton yard to its namesake Leicestershire mine. Class 58s were notoriously difficult to keep clean due to their narrow, modular bodies, which traditional washing plants couldn't reach to clean. 31 January 1997.

On this lovely summer's day I was train watching from Long Tom footbridge when a pair of Class 37s came off the shed and went into the Up yard, and with nothing booked to do this I knew it had to be for a special. So a quick call to a colleague at work confirmed that Nos 37377 and 37370 would work 6Z69 13.59 to Croft quarry. They are seen climbing the high-level line, with Long Tom footbridge framing the train. 26 July 1999.

The small group of Class 60s, which were adorned with the Mainline Freight aircraft blue livery, were always worth looking out for, as they were a welcome change to the standard triple grey Mainline livery that proliferated around the area. No. 60011 is seen shortly after departing New Bank with 7A15 14.45 Toton Yard–Ratcliffe power station. 4 October 1996.

BR blue-liveried No. 31467 takes the high-level goods line at Toton Junction with Target 89 trip, running on this day as 8T89 08.15 Stapleford & Sandiacre-Nottingham Eastcroft with a rail crane for maintenance. The Toton area trip workings generally worked every weekday with T89 usually running to/from and shunting at Chaddesden yard (on this day No. 31467 ran light to Chaddesden from Eastcroft), with T91/92/93 trips working any other requirements such as ad-hoc loading of engineers wagons with ballast from the East Midlands quarries. 9 June 1997.

No. 45048 *THE ROYAL MARINES* takes the Up high-level goods at Toton Junction with a York to Loughborough ballast train. 25 April 1984. (G. Griffiths)

No. 25089 arrives at Toton with a Speedlink working and crosses from the Down high-level goods to enter the North yard via the west arrival line over the flyover and the Down side hump. 27 August 1985. This route over the flyover was abolished on 30 March 1986, with the box at Toton East junction closing on 27 September 1985. (A. Walker)

Original Peak No. 44004, by now de-named, passes Long Tom footbridge on the Down main with a mixed freight made up of two vacuum-braked 21-ton coal hoppers, a 12-ton vacuum-braked van, four vacuum-braked 22-ton tube wagons, three plank open wagon, three 32-ton HAA air-braked coal hoppers and a 20-ton brake van. 28 April 1978. (J. Woolley)

No. 31213 is exiting West yard and crossing the switch diamonds of Toton Junction, taking the route towards Trent East Junction with a mixed freight. No. 31285 and a Class 08 can be seen in West Yard, and another Class 08 pilot is busy in the East yard. 8 June 1983. (A. Walker).

No. 47635 *The Lass O'Ballochmyle* is departing from Toton with 6G78 12.16 to Bescot yard. This was the last leg of a three-part service that started ex-Bescot, serving Burton yard. It then carried on to Toton, with the final leg then heading back to Bescot. 17 December 2003.

A de-named No. 45044 takes the Up high-level goods at Toton Junction with an MGR bound for Staythorpe power station. 31 May 1985. (A. Walker)

No. 58018 drifts down the high-level goods to Toton Junction with a set of MGR empties from Ratcliffe power station, just visible in the distance through the murky light. 25 September 1985. (PR Collection)

In the autumn of 2018, much to the delight of local photographers the usually DB Cargo-operated RHTT programme based from Toton was outsourced to Colas Railfreight. Here 3J88 04.17 Toton–Crewe-Worksop–Lincoln–Nottingham–Grantham–Toton RHTT arrives back at base with No. 56090 leading and No. 56094 tailing. 4 October 2018.

No. 56088 wearing, in my opinion, the best livery to adorn a *Grid*, descends the Down high-level goods line from Toton East Junction with a Speedlink service bound for the Old Bank, consisting of HEA coal hoppers and VAA vans. 31 May 1985. (A. Walker)

InterCity-liveried No. 37152 descends the high-level goods line with 6P55 14.41 Norwich Crown Point depot–Toton Old Bank, conveying fuel oil empties for return to Lindsey OR. This was a Class 31 duty, so to my eyes the allocation of the former Scottish 37 was an upgrade at the time. 21 August 1995.

BR blue heaven as No. 47317 draws out of Long Eaton oil terminal, being overtaken by No. 25205 on the Down main line with a mixed goods, as No. 56042, with its experimental bogies, departs from the Independent line with a loaded MGR bound for Ratcliffe. 15 July 1983. (A. Walker)

In stark contrast to the 1983 view, modernisation has seen a sea change in motive power, and coal wagons, and the infrastructure has been rationalised and resignalled. The wagons works, now closed, awaits demolition. Note the running gear from HAA wagons as seen behind the Class 56 in the older picture now sit below the ballast wagons in the modern picture – it's good to recycle! No. 66511 waits acceptance into the North yard with a loaded ballast train from Bardon Hill as No. 60007 *The Spirit of Tom Kendell* departs with 6Z18 14.45 Ratcliffe power station–Warrington Walton Old Junction. 30 January 2012.

A fairly new to traffic No. 58025 takes the high-level goods at Toton Junction, towards Meadow Lane Junction, conveying a single Bromine chemical tanker, plus brakevan. 11 March 1985. (J. Mattison/PR Collection)

No. 25297 departs from Toton underneath a threatening sky and takes the Up high-level goods line at Toton Junction. The consist is three Railfreight VCA vans thought to have originated from the Metal Box factory at Kirkby in Ashfield. 19 September 1983. (C. Smith)

No. 60008 *GYPSUM QUEEN II* in the attractive load haul orange and black livery departs Toton with 6Z32 08.00 Toton North yard–Mountsorrel for loading with ballast for the Toton virtual quarry. 23 July 1999.

No. 47758 departs with 6T18 08.33 Toton Yard–Chaddesden Yard spoil, a train that would normally be Class 37 hauled, but could also chuck out Class 31s, 47s or 58s in this era. 24 April 2002.

No. 37025 *Inverness TMD* tails a PLPR test train, led by No. 37421, along the Down goods line, running as 1Q64 08.52 Derby RTC–Neville Hill, which runs on a six-weekly basis. The vegetation growing between the main lines and the former Down hump now hides the fact that there was ever a railway there at all. 25 June 2018.

The diversion of the Southampton–Leeds and v/v Freightliner services via the Erewash Valley has provided more interest through Toton in recent years, with three trains in each direction in daylight during the summer months, now supplemented by other container trains to/from Masborough, Doncaster i-Port and East Midlands Gateway. Here Nos 70010 and 66559 pass through with 4O90 06.10 Leeds FLT–Southampton MT. 15 June 2019.

Nos 20159 and 20198 pass through Toton on the Up Main with a loaded, unfitted coal train made up almost exclusively of 21-ton coal hoppers. 1 September 1980. (J. Woolley).

Departmental grey and yellow-liveried (known as Dutch) No. 37106 has just taken the Up high-level goods line at Toton Junction with 8F10 08.27 Stapleford and Sandiacre–Mountsorrel empty ballast, a train that was a daily sight until the advent of the virtual quarry concept. 18 May 1998.

The Corby 'tubeliner' was an impressive train to look out for at Toton, bringing pairs of Thornaby-allocated Class 37s on hot rolled coil through the area. On this day Nos 37096 and 37042 pass Toton Junction with 6M47 10.50 Lackenby-Corby. 6 March 1985. (C. Smith)

The short-lived Jarvis Fastline Freight operation worked regular flows of coal from Daw Mill and Hatfield to Ratcliffe power station, with both flows regularly passing through or running round at Toton. Here No. 66301 is seen passing the now closed wagon shops with the 6A59 12.32 Hatfield colliery–Ratcliffe coal. 29 April 2009.

No. 47790 *Galloway Princess* top-and-tailing with No. 57307 *Lady Penelope* passes Toton with the Northern Belle charter running as 1Z94 08.17 Edinburgh–London St Pancras. 29 July 2014.

Following railtour duties and overnight stabling in Toton yard, English Electric Class 50s Nos 50049 *Defiance* and 50031 *Hood* depart from Toton with 5Z66 09.15 Toton–Old Oak Common ECS. 11 October 2004.

HNRC-liveried No. 20311, paired with Railfreight grey No. 20132 top-and-tailing with No. 66724 *Drax Power Station*, departs Toton on a diverted 7X08 14.54 Derby Litchurch Lane–West Ruislip 'S' stock transfer. The train ran via Toton to reverse on several occasions due to the remodelling of Derby station. 25 August 2018. (T. Robertson)

In extremely lucky lighting, DRS large logo Class 37 Nos 37407 and 37403 *Isle of Mull* pass through Toton with 6Z37 12.10 Shirebrook WH Davies–Crewe Coal sidings conveying eight new FNA nuclear flask covered wagons. 7 February 2019.

A late-running 6K50 15.13 Toton yard–Crewe Basford Hall ambles off the Independent line with a multi-coloured quadruple header. Freightliner's No. 66587 *AS ONE, WE CAN* leads classmate No. 66554, and DB Cargo-operated Nos 66044 and 66051 *Maritime Intermodal Four* are also hitching a lift as the first tints of autumn show themselves in the plentiful foliage growing where there used to be sidings. 21 September 2020. (T. Robertson)

No. 40080 is viewed passing light engine under the 'Little Tom' footbridge. It's amazing to see how the original housing estate in Toton had a clear view over to the sidings. 15 July 1983. (A. Walker)

BR green-liveried No. 08332 is seen from the top of the 'Little Tom' footbridge, shunting a rake of loaded coal/coke wagons into the East yard, fan no. 3. The wagons are a mixture of vacuum-brake fitted and unfitted 16-ton minerals and 21-ton hoppers. There has been a vast change here with almost all of the infrastructure and buildings visible having been closed and lifted or demolished. 28 April 1978. (J. Woolley)

English Electric Class 40 No. 40195 eases out of Toton East yard and passes over the River Erewash bridge (which remains today, minus the concrete handrails) with a coal train formed of 21t HTV hoppers, seen from the base of the 'Little Tom' footbridge. This Class 40 became one of the most photographed Whistlers four years later, being on the end of the scrap line at the Crewe works open day with its bonnet doors open. 26 September 1983. (C. Smith)

No. 08027 brings a varied assortment of wagons on the wagon works tripper, including four 16-ton minerals loaded with coal that may be for use at the wagon works, rather than these requiring repairs themselves. No. 08027 transferred from Derby to Toton in May 1968, where it would remain in use until it was withdrawn in November 1980, being scrapped at Swindon Works in April 1982. 28 April 1978. (J. Woolley)

No. 08181 shunts a busy looking wagon works yard, with a good variety of cars on show in the staff car park, 28 April 1978. The works was closed by EWS in the mid-2000s, and unfortunately became a vandalised, fire-damaged ruin – though there was a chance of rebirth when a submission was made to use the location as a concrete sleeper making plant. This was rejected by the local council due to environmental and road access issues. The building was finally demolished in 2018. (J. Woolley)

The works was generally served twice daily in the late 1990s. Here No. 08495 handles the teatime wagon works tripper, seen from the former flyover trackbed. 4 June 1997.

Inside the wagon works, this was a regular scene over Christmas periods with main line locomotives stabled to protect them from the elements during the shutdown. Here seven Class 20s and a pair of original Peaks headed by No. 44007 are seen on 24 December 1979. (PR Collection)

A busy moment at Toton sees No. 56006 departing New Bank with an MGR for Ratcliffe power station; No. 37274 in Old Bank with a Speedlink coal working; and No. 47359 passing on the Down main with oil empties from the Long Eaton terminal. 25 May 1990. (PR Collection)

A good view is afforded across the yard from the bank, showing the West yard, Toton Centre signalbox, and the Up hump buildings as new No. 56012 passes on an empty MGR. 31 August 1977. (PR Collection)

One of the investments made by EWS at Toton was the reinstatement of the south end connections to New Bank sidings 7–11. Here No. 56112 *Stainless Pioneer* is seen using one of these while it waits to form 6T21 10.50 to Oxcroft (via Derby). When the infrastructure at Toton was reviewed in subsequent years to enable cost savings, New Bank was abandoned to all but storage of unwanted assets, and these sidings were once again made dead end roads with the removal of the track and pointwork from all but the closest line. 27 June 2002.

During EWS's tenure, the use of Class 08 and 09 shunt locos was wound down and eventually ousted in favour of using main line locomotives. Class 60s have become commonplace on these duties at Toton, and at dawn on 19 December 2008, No. 60051 is seen pausing between movements in Old Bank yard.

No. 58044 *Oxcroft Opencast* rests in New Bank prior to working 7A15 08.47 to Ratcliffe power station. In the foreground a long line of redundant Type 2 locomotives are headed by Nos 31290, 31294, 31116 and 31184. 14 August 1997.

No. 58044 *Oxcroft Opencast* is glimpsed between withdrawn Class 31 locos Nos 31294 and 31116 in Toton New Bank. 14 August 1997.

Fast forward two decades from the shots with the redundant Class 31s stored in New Bank, and the yard itself is now abandoned apart from the storage of various wagons, and rusting members of the class of loco that rendered the 31s obsolete! The longer line of sixteen locos is headed by triple grey-liveried Nos 60067, 60032 and 60088, with another line of eleven of the class further along the yard. 21 April 2020.

No. 08711 in parcels red livery is the Up side pilot on 7 April 2008, busy shuffling a YJB crane around. Visible in the background are stored Nos 37406, 37410, 37416 and 60088 on the south apron of the depot.

Mainline blue liveried No. 58038 departs from New Bank and descends the former up side hump with 6T48 08.35 empties to Nadins disposal point. In the background is one of Toton's most infamous residents, long withdrawn No. 45015 which managed to survive as long as early 2022 before being scrapped, without ever being restored. It was latterly stored at the Battlefield railway. 12 August 1997.

A dusting of snow has fallen on Toton overnight. No. 08783 is resting in Old Bank as No. 66049 departs New Bank with 6Z87 04.35 Immingham–Rugeley power station. 27 February 2004.

No. 37308 in its celebrity BR blue livery spent a period working from Toton in spring 2003, and while at work one afternoon I noted it was allocated to work 7E15 22.29 to Whitemoor. Therefore, my journey home was delayed by a late visit, where luckily the loco was stood in a lit position in Old Bank yard. 7 April 2003.

No. 40022, formerly named *Laconia*, has just arrived on the New Bank at Toton with 8M20 from Healey Mills. 22 December 1981. (G. Griffiths, B&W photo colourised by S. Arrandale)

No. 40145 stands in Toton yard with 6E75 from Willesden Brent to Leeds as the yard Class 08 pilot busies itself. 19 February 1983. (G. Griffiths)

No. 56049 stands in Toton Old Bank with 6A83 for Willesden. 9 March 1983. (G. Griffiths)

No. 40050 has just arrived in the Old Bank with 6E95 from Warrington Arpley. March 1983. (G. Griffiths)

In sparkling condition following release from a CEM overhaul at Toton, No. 56094 *Eggborough Power Station* stands in New Bank with 6T28 07.55 to Hicks Lodge. 12 August 1998.

Toton Down side control tower, standing derelict and awaiting its fate as No. 58019 *Shirebrook Colliery* creeps by. Hump shunting ceased on the Down side in March 1978, with the tower remaining in situ until the year 2000. 5 February 1993.

I visited the former operating floor of the Down side tower on a couple of occasions, though it was rather nerve wracking on your own as there was evidence of drug use taking place there by this time. Here looking north, No. 60079 *Foinaven* is departing with 7V06 12.48 Toton to Didcot power station, passing rakes of Speedlink coal wagons and MGRs in the West yard. 2 February 1995.

Looking to the south, the driver of No. 58003 *Markham Colliery* has stopped as required at the stop board to contact the yard for instructions on where to deposit 6A51 11.49 from Ratcliffe power station. The hump and former arrival lines remain amazingly clear of vegetation, but this has now long since succumbed to a veritable jungle. 2 February 1995.

The New Bank yard and Up side hump are eerily quiet due to this shot being taken on the fourth of fifteen consecutive days of industrial action by ASLEF drivers, striking over hours of work. Note the hump signals, known as 'Toton signals', which would only illuminate when humping was taking place. These could show three light configurations, either horizontally (stop humping), diagonally (hump slow) or vertically (hump normal). The wing application lights – AKA 'ears' – lit with one lamp to indicate which siding the hump signal referred to, when a signal was shared between the two sidings it stood between. 7 July 1982. (P. Kazmierczak).

The former National Power-operated fleet of Class 59/2s settled down to working aggregates trains from the Mendips, but DB Schenker trialled them on other flows, including coal out of Liverpool docks. No. 59201 made it to the East Midlands on this day with such a train from Liverpool and waits to work the next leg, 6Z87 18.40 Toton to Ratcliffe power station, unusually laying over on the independent line rather than in the yard. 20 April 2010.

No. 58050 *Toton Traction Depot* comes over the remains of the former Up side hump as it begins its journey with 6T17 07.42 Toton New Bank–Daw Mill colliery. 27 April 2000.

No. 60040 *The Territorial Army Centenary* stands in North yard, top-and-tail on a possession train with a Class 66. A DRS Class 68 in Chiltern livery can also be seen in the yard having just arrived on 6D95 from Bescot yard. 12 June 2018. (C. Adamson)

Whilst Toton has always been littered with stored and withdrawn locos waiting to be taken away for scrapping, it wasn't very often that any scrapping actually took place on site. However, there have been exceptions and in 2004 some work was carried out by contractors within the former CM&EE compound. This view sees former Class 37s (which were converted for moving loco engines around the depot whilst being overhauled) awaiting their turn for the cutters torch. EC1 (formerly No. 37070) and EC2 (formerly No. 37138) are next in line, whilst the remains of classmate No. 37343 (formerly No. 37049) litter the left foreground. More recently No. 60006 met its end at Toton, and withdrawn parcels vehicles and wagons that were littering the closed up side yards have also been scrapped on site. 18 February 2004.

A long-standing feature of the North yard was the long line of withdrawn Class 45s (and several
Class 25s) totalling twenty-five locos. Here the north end of the line is seen headed by No. 45006,
with the five Peaks visible behind being Nos 45102/077/101/123 and 131. 12 September 1987.

No. 25151 was another long-term resident in the 'playpen', being used for rerailing exercises
for the Toton breakdown crew. The accident damage to the loco occurred on 3 September 1982
when it lost control of a freight near Huddersfield and collided with a ferry van, when it was
diverted into a siding by the signaller to protect the main line. 28 May 1985. (J. Freebury)

For a period in 2014, GBRf experimented with loco combinations on some of the local infrastructure services. These were locos that the company had hired in to supplement their Class 66 fleet and here a combination of Riviera Trains' No. 47843 *VULCAN* and HNRC's No. 20118 *Saltburn-by-the-Sea* are seen in Toton North yard after arrival with 6D51 from Crewe Basford Hall. 4 April 2014. (J. Mosley)

BR blue-liveried Class 56 No. 56022 is seen arriving at Toton Down yard with a set of MGR empties from Ratcliffe power station. 5 February 1993.

No. 25060 departs from Toton West yard with T12 trip for Derby St Marys. Note the shunters gloves atop the lamp irons! 17 April 1984. (G. Griffiths)

DB Cargo operated No. 60066 and Colas Rail Freight operated No. 56302 *PECO The Railway Modeller 2016 70 years* stand in Toton Old Bank yard with engineering trains, the Class 56 being prepared to depart with a Railvac train bound for a ballast renewal site at Sileby. 13 August 2016. (C. Adamson)

In the spring of 2022, DB Cargo opened a car terminal on the land where the former CM&EE compound had been situated between North yard and Meadow sidings. Up to three trains per week are exporting Toyota vehicles produced at Burnaston near Derby, and they also back load from France with other Toyota models that are not built in the UK. The train is split into two sidings for loading/unloading and here No. 66125 is backing into the sidings with the second portion of 6X13 02.22 from Dollands Moor. Note the recently cleared West yard on the left. 30 April 2022.

In stunning lighting conditions, Class 58 No. 58050 departs from Toton North yard, passing the arrival and departure connections to the depot with 6T02 20.53 MGR empties to Bentinck colliery. 10 June 1998.

No. 37370 has just arrived on the Independent line at Toton with 8T01 15.00 loaded pipes from Stanton. The train will be propelled into Old Bank yard to be coupled to another rake of pipes brought down earlier in the day, forming a fully loaded train for export via Goole Docks. 21 February 2000.

No. 67008 is acting as the yard pilot and is about to reverse at Toton Centre with a short train of IFA tilting wagons on an Old Bank to North yard transfer. 27 March 2018. (C. Adamson)

No. 66056, still wearing full EWS livery, is the Meadow sidings virtual quarry pilot and is seen drawing an empty set of wagons out of the spoil road. Image captured with a drone. 1 September 2020.

Belmond Royal Scotsman-liveried No. 66746 stands in Meadow sidings with 6F46 01.54 ballast empties to Stud Farm quarry. Note the positioning of the loco number within the puddle by the photographer! 11 December 2018. (J. Mosley)

No. 47843 *VULCAN* has a dead No. 57312 *Peter Henderson* in tow as it waits to leave Toton Old Bank yard with 6K50 15.13 to Crewe Basford Hall. 28 March 2014. (J. Mosley)

No. 66719 *METRO-LAND* is standing on the Independent line at Toton with 6K50 15.13 Toton to Crewe Basford Hall. 12 November 2013. (J. Mosley)

DRS-operated No. 68016 *Fearless* has arrived at Toton with 4K97 from Bescot, conveying the Wigan-based crane and breakdown vans that were en route to Ely, where a GBRf container train had derailed on the Ely North curve. 15 August 2017. (C. Adamson)

During the engineering blockade for the remodelling of Derby station in the summer of 2018, several movements of the LUL 'S' stock to and from Litchurch Lane works were diverted via Spondon and a reversal at Toton, to reach the Burton route via Castle Donington. Here No. 20096 *Ian Goddard 1938–2016* and No. 20107 are waiting a path to drop down to Toton Centre to reverse and head back south to run over the Castle Donington branch. The train ran as 7X08 16.55 Derby Litchurch Lane–West Ruislip. 24 July 2018. (J. Mosley)

No. 60020 *The Willows* sits in Old Bank yard with a an imported steel train from Boston Docks, bound for Wolverhampton steel terminal – the steel bound for use in the motor industry. The train had departed Old Bank in the early hours, but failed on approach to Trent East Junction, and was dragged back to the yard by a Class 66. A fitter was working on the loco when this view was taken by drone, and the train successfully departed with the Class 60, now well again, within the hour. 22 August 2020.

Open days at Toton depot have always been popular events, drawing large crowds of both enthusiasts and curious locals to see what happens at the UKs largest diesel maintenance depot. It's fair to say that as the years have passed health and safety has put a dampener on proceedings. At this open day No. 44008 *PENYGHENT* was used for giving cab rides in Meadow sidings at a princely sum of ten pence per trip! 9 June 1979. (PR Collection)

Toton residents Nos 58043, 58021 and 58012 are seen on the shed front in the company of a very clean Class 08, as enthusiasts enjoy another Toton open day. 4 May 1987. (PR Collection)

The final Class 58 built by BREL Doncaster was delivered to Toton with modifications to its traction equipment (SEPEX wheelslip control system), which saw it lay idle at the depot for testing and training for quite some while. Here it is seen at an open day at the south end of the shed, yet to be named after its home depot. 4 May 1987. (PR Collection)

The last open day to date at Toton was actually a two-day affair, jointly arranged by EWS and *RAIL* magazine. On the south end apron, a selection of preserved power was lined up, and here Nos D200, D172 *Ixion* and 45060 *Sherwood Forester* stand in the morning sunshine during a photographers 'early bird' event, prior to the masses being allowed entry! 29 August 1998.

At the August 1998 open weekend, this line up at the south end of the depot consisted of Nos 37258, 50015 *Valiant*, D1023 *WESTERN FUSILIER*, D444, D5500, 5580 and on the far right No. 47484 *ISAMBARD KINGDOM BRUNEL*. There were a further three locos behind me here – No. 26004 with No. 27001, plus No. 50033 *Glorious* against the buffer stops. 29 August 1998.

During the open weekend in 1998, a collection of Class 47s were displayed around the fuel point area. No. 47004 *Old Oak Common Traction & Rolling Stock Depot* has No. 47799 *Prince Henry* on the same line behind it, with No. 47798 *Prince William* on the adjacent line. Also out of shot to the right were No. 47114 *Freightlinerbulk* and No. 47484 *ISAMBARD KINGDOM BRUNEL*. 29 August 1998.

Following the end of Class 58 operations in the UK, a small number of the class were hired to Dutch freight operator ACTS. It was originally envisaged that a fleet of five would 'go Dutch', but only three actually made the move. No. 5811, the former No. 58039, is seen on release from the paint booth in ACTS blue and yellow livery ahead of being dragged to Immingham docks the following day by No. 60081. The second loco to be exported was No. 5812 (No. 58044), which moved to Holland later in 2003. 24 June 2003.

Here the former No. 58038 has been repainted in VOS Logistics livery and renumbered No. 5814, seen next to No. 60095 just prior to movement to Immingham for shipping out to Holland. ACTS dispensed with using the Class 58s in March 2009, and they were repainted and moved to join other ex-pat Class 58s in France being used on the Rhine-Rhone LGV construction project. The former No. 58038 currently remains stored in southern France with little chance of it or its classmates seeing any further use. 29 April 2005.

Nos. 73128 and 73131 were sent to Toton for repaints in the autumn of 1999 ahead of some planned Royal train work. No. 73128 was deemed to be in good condition paint wise so did not receive a full repaint; No. 73131, however, did need the full treatment and is seen in the paint booth being filled, sanded and prepped ready for a new application of red and gold. 29 September 1999.

No. 90024 has something of an affiliation with Toton paint shop, having visited for repaints on at least three occasions. Here the loco was being unveiled to the press after being repainted in First Scotrail 'Barbie' colours for use on the Caledonian sleeper services. The loco has also been painted into GNER blue and its current Malcolm Logistics colours at Toton. 10 June 2006.

Unveiled to the railway press on a day blessed with sunny skies, No. 37419 and No. 37670 *St Blazey T & RS Depot* sparkle in their new coats of DB Schenker red alongside the paint shop. Neither saw a huge amount of use after being repainted; No. 37670s internal condition caught up with it and it had a significant engine failure in October, and No. 37419 was sold on to DRS (with its other 37/4 classmates) in 2010. 23 July 2009.

No. 89001 *Avocet*, aka 'The Badger', gleams in the autumn sunshine after being repainted into INTERCITY colours in Toton paint shop, as part of its revival to main line operational status. It stands with former ECR Class 66s Nos 66211 and 66247, with No. 60091 *Barry Needham* stood alongside. 22 September 2020. (C. Adamson).

Original pilot scheme Peak Class 44 No. D6 *Whernside* is seen wearing BR green with full yellow ends, basking in the afternoon sunshine on the north apron of the shed. 17 October 1971. (J. Freebury).

Peak Class 45 No. 64 *COLDSTREAM GUARDSMAN* stands outside no. 1 road at the south end of the shed on the afternoon of 19 January 1969. (J. Freebury)

Stabled on the shed front in this view are Brush Type 4 No. 1617 and EE Type 1 No. 8176. The D prefixes in front of the loco numbers having been discontinued and removed or painted over. These two locos had differing fates with No. 1617 still in service to this day with West Coast Railways as No. 47760, while the Class 20 became No. 20176, being withdrawn from service in October 1991 and scrapped at MC Metals Glasgow in early 1994. 14 March 1971. (PR Collection)

I spy a Class 27. Stabled at the north end of the shed at Toton are a glut of EE Type 1 locos including the pioneer No. D8000 (later renumbered No. 20050 and now part of the national collection) and No. D8192, identified by its running number being stencilled onto the buffer beam. Furthest from the camera viewed between the bonnets is BRCW Class 27 No. D5386, which was only ten months away from migrating north of the border to Eastfield. The loco would later receive three different TOPS numbers in it's BR career: Nos 27103, 27212 and finally 27066. The loco was saved after withdrawal and saw use in preservation but currently is awaiting restoration again and can be found at Barrow Hill. 19 January 1969. (J. Freebury).

Type 2 Class 25 Nos 5239 and 5241 stand on the shed front, *c*. 1972. (PR Collection)

A pair of original Peak Class 44s stand on the fuel road awaiting attention. Closest to the camera is No. 44008 *Penyghent*. 5 March 1976. (PR Collection)

No. 40013 formerly named *Andania* rests on the shed front at Toton between No. 45044 and a Class 31. Following withdrawal in October 1984, No. 40013 was bulled up with silver window surrounds, a white bodyside stripe and red buffer beams, and was used as an exhibition loco. The loco passed into preservation in 1988, and has been returned to main line standard, being currently operated Locomotive Services Ltd. (PR Collection).

South Wales-allocated No. 37187 is an unusual visitor to Toton on this day, really looking the part in weathered BR blue with miniature snow ploughs, buffer skirts, domino headcodes and frost shields. (PR Collection)

No. 40122 was chosen to become a celebrity railtour loco, having extensive work undertaken at Toton to return it to operational condition, painted in original green livery as No. D200. Here the loco is seen undergoing the work, with the application of green undercoat ongoing. 11 June 1983. (N. Young)

Standing on the wheel lathe road, Whistler No. 40192 awaits its turn for its wheel sets to be attended to. 4 November 1984. (PR Collection)

A weekend permit visit to Toton in the early 1980s sees power laid up ready for the following week. English Electric Whistler No. 40118 heads a line of four Class 20s, the closest here being No. 20187. Alongside is a clean early series Class 56. (PR Collection)

The last of the BTH Class 15s had been withdrawn by BR in March 1971 , with four of them transferred to the departmental fleet for carriage heating duties. This was only a short-lived life extension, and ADB968002, the former No. D8237, was laid up at Toton for some months before moving to Marple & Gillot of Sheffield for breaking in 1985. The loco is seen in the north head shunt with withdrawn Class 40 No. 40073 and an unidentified Class 08. (PR Collection)

No. 56098 is at the forefront of this typical view of the cabs outside the shed, the line-up containing members of classes 25, 37 (both headcode variants), 45, 47 and 56. 1 September 1984. (PR Collection)

Seen in typical BR condition, in typical summer weather conditions, No. 45112 *THE ROYAL ARMY ORDNANCE CORPS* stands outside the shed with No. 25072. No. 45137 *THE BEDFORDSHIRE AND HERTFORDSHIRE REGIMENT (T.A.)* can be glimpsed in the background. 14 June 1986.

Showing the original loco wash plant, Nos 47357, 45116 and 45115 stand waiting their next duties during a Saturday shed visit by official BR depot permit. 14 June 1986.

A selection of BR blue-liveried power is seen from the cab of withdrawn No. 25032, with No. 45116 closest to the camera. 14 June 1986.

Stabled on the north apron are Nos 47285, 47222 *Appleby Frodingham*, 20094, 20108 and 45137 *THE BEDFORDSHIRE AND HERTFORDSHIRE REGIMENT (T.A.)*, with withdrawn No. 25032 and No. 45074 visible in the distance. 14 June 1986.

In the original Railfreight grey large logo livery, No. 47280 *Pedigree* is standing on the fuel point and awaits a shunt driver to move it onto the front of the shed to await its next duty. (PR Collection)

Large logo grey rules in this view, with Nos 58030, 58024, and 58005 lined up, with a Class 56 on the adjacent road. (PR Collection)

On the shed front on a fine June morning the photographer has captured Nos 45019 and 46023. The 46 was the standby loco for the Old Dalby staged nuclear flask crash that took place the previous year, with No. 46009 meeting its end in the experiment. 15 June 1985. (PR Collection)

Romanian-built No. 56013, in Railfreight triple grey with coal sector decals, sits inside the shed awaiting attention. 25 October 1992.

Type 5 power lined up within the shed, with Nos 56107, 56132, 58033 and 56077 all undergoing maintenance. 25 October 1992.

Nos 56020 and 56061 are seen inside the shed undergoing A exams. 25 October 1992.

Looking in the opposite direction sees Nos 58026 and 56022 also standing on the through roads while undergoing A exams. 25 October 1992.

No. 56133 *Crewe Locomotive Works* is seen undergoing a CEM light overhaul. 26 February 1994.

During the run down of the Class 31 fleet, the south end of the shed became a holding point for stored locomotives. Seen here from left to right are Nos 31531, 31149, 31247 and 31541. 29 July 1995.

An interloper from the southern region could be found in the shed on this day, with stored BRCW Class 33 No. 33029 seen here not long after arrival. No. 58008 had brought the Crompton up from Hither Green earlier that morning, with the purpose of the transfer reputedly being to allow fitters to gain experience on the type ahead of a possible refurbishment programme for the Class 33 fleet. This was not forthcoming, and No. 33029 littered various sidings around the site for several years prior to being purchased and overhauled by DRS. The loco is currently owned by WCRC. 29 July 1995.

Four locos from four different loco types allocated to Toton are seen in this view, with Nos 58037, 31163, 37293 and a Class 60 awaiting their turn to receive attention inside the shed. 26 April 1998.

Although at this time it was not unusual to find Cross Country Class 47s on shed, with EWS having gained the contract for maintenance of the fleet, Midland Mainline HSTs were somewhat rarer. In this view No. 47805 awaits its turn in the wheel lathe bay, waiting for the HST set, with No. 43058 poking out of the shed, to finish being tyre turned. 12 March 1998.

EE Type 3 power is the main traction on the shed front on this day, with Nos 37686, EC1 & EC2, 37153, 37131 and 37431 in view. 29 May 1999.

After attending a press call for No. 90024 being repainted into GNER blue, and finding the loco still being painted in the paint booth, the depot manager agreed that I could return the next morning to see the finished article. Following a night shift, I made my way to the depot in lovely sunshine, only to find the loco was now complete, but was hidden inside the main shed – the foreman not having been told I was coming. I was sent to the fitters mess room to wait whilst they found a driver to shunt several locos out of the way to put the gleaming Class 90 out in the sunshine for me, and this was the resulting shot. with Nos 56118 and 58013 for company. 29 May 1999.

No. 56081 is seen being coupled up to Class 58s Nos 58022, 58017 *Eastleigh Depot* and 58018 *High Marnham Power Station*, and these would shortly depart as 0D02 11.30 to Doncaster via Worksop with the Class 58s destined for storage. 28 May 1999.

The former No. 37138, which had lain withdrawn at Toton along with classmate No. 37070, were chosen to become internal user vehicles for moving loco engines around the shed while overhauls took place. They originally had crude gaps cut into the bodysides just around the engine area, but this was later extended to be cab to cab as seen here. EC2 (No. 37138) is seen in the company of No. 37686 on the north end of the depot, however the concept was short lived and the use of them dwindled, with both EC1 and EC2 being scrapped on site in February 2004. 29 May 1999.

A storm on the shed has recently cleared, leaving some lovely light to pick out No. 58015 and stored No. 37275 on the shed front. 29 September 1999.

A typical varied line-up of cab ends is seen on the shed front with Nos 37351, 58048, 47285 and 56011 to the fore. Class 60s and 66s are the most likely to be seen now in the present day. 27 February 1999.

Still showing the staining received whilst on a stint on the weed killing train, BR blue celebrity No. 37308 is hooked up to the Toton load bank equipment. One of the joys of living locally was being able to clearly hear the older locomotives being thrashed mercilessly on here, morning, noon and night! 14 June 2004. (C. Adamson)

English Electric Class 37 locos Nos 37422 *Cardiff Canton* and 37416 *The Royal Scotsman* are seen on the lifting roads with No. 37416 lifted clear of its bogies, which is always an impressive sight to see with a loco raised up on the jacks. 13 October 2005. (C. Adamson)

Class 60 No. 60078 *Stac Pollaidh* and stored Class 56 No. 56028 are seen inside the shed on the lifting roads. The Class 56 would never work again. The Class 60 would remain in traffic until July 2007 before being stored, and is currently dumped in New Bank. 26 February 1994.

The fuel roads at Toton are seen with No. 66183 having arrived for a top up, whilst alongside are withdrawn Class 08 Nos 08561 and 08466, plus stored Class 60 Nos 60055 *Thomas Barnado*, 60082 and 60061. No. 60055 had a second coming, being sold to DCR, and being overhauled and returned to use by DB at Toton in 2019, whilst early in 2022 No. 60061 was also sold to DCR along with several other Class 60s. 23 July 2009.

In this view Nos 56099, 56134 and 56048 are stored out of use, and had been brought from Immingham to Toton for possible use in the export hire contract for Fertis, which did not come to fruition for these locos. No. 37717 Berwick Middle School Railsafe Trophy Winners 1998 can be seen between the Grids. 29 April 2005.

The south end of the shed remains a holding area to this day, with locos waiting attention, or for parts to arrive, or stored awaiting a decision on their future. Here stored Nos 67003, 60099, 66145 and 60038 stand with Nos 66187, 60066 and a DB red Class 66 awaiting attention on 8 March 2020. (C. Adamson).

A view across the north end of the shed and fuelling point with DB's core fleet of classes 60s, 66 and 67 on show. Left to right: Nos 67019, 67006 *Royal Sovereign*, 66144, 60011, 66133, 66066 *Geoff Spencer*, 66198, 66101, and 60024 *Clitheroe Castle*. 7 July 2018. (C. Adamson)

On a glorious September evening, the inhabitants of Toton TMD and Stapleford & Sandiacre sidings are seen from the drone. Locos that can be picked out from the crowd include DCR's No. 60029 *Ben Nevis*, DCR Cappagh blue-liveried No. 60028, Royal Train loco No. 67006 *Royal Sovereign* and unique electric loco No. 89001 *Avocet*. 13 September 2020.

A few days later and the shed is viewed from the south-east side with the drone, showing the stored locos on the south apron, and locos waiting for attention inside the shed on the north apron, again including No. 89001 *Avocet*. The high output ballast cleaner train (HOBC) is also seen stabled in Stapleford & Sandiacre sidings. 16 September 2020.

An overall view of the shed and stabling sidings are seen in this view, with a total of fifty-two locos on view made up of two Class 67s, thirteen Class 60s and thirty-seven Class 66s. 12 July 2020.

Viewed from the A52 bridge Sulzer Type 2 Class 25 No. 25293 arrives at Toton with 9Z04 Sunday engineers service. Note the line of Class 44 Peak locos outstabled in Old Bank yard. At weekends when space was tight on shed due to the sheer amount of locos present, the Class 44s were often moved over to Old Bank ready for work on the Monday morning. 21 April 1974. (PR Collection)

Two-tone green-liveried No. D1828 departs from Toton with an empty mineral train, which has probably originated from Meadow sidings. On shed are members of classes 20, 25, 44, 45 and 47, with a Class 44 also waiting to come off shed. Under the BR Tops scheme, No. D1828 became No. 47347, and in 1999 the loco was rebuilt as No. 57004. 26 July 1973. (PR Collection)

Nos 37899 and 37719 depart from Toton North yard with 7Z72 14.00 Bardon Hill–Doncaster Decoy yard conveying boulders for sea defence works in the Hull area. The train had called into North yard to attach the two cargo-waggon flats seen behind the locos, with the train finally setting off for Doncaster in nice late spring evening light. 24 May 1999.

Freightliner-operated No. 66622 departs from Toton Centre after a crew change, working 6M84 13.06 Dagenham–Earles empty bogie cement tanks. Plenty of Class 60 and 66 power can be seen on the shed front awaiting attention. 5 June 2020.

The view from the north side of the A52 bridge sees No. 66726 in the attractive GBRf 'Barbie' colour scheme passing Stapleford and Sandiacre shunt frame with 6A59 12.50 Hatfield colliery–Ratcliffe power station, a service operated by Jarvis Fastline Freight. When they first began operating coal trains in 2008, they hired in Class 66s from GBRf and DRS until all of their own locomotives, Nos 66301–305, were in use. Even then they still had a requirement to occasionally hire in additional locos, as was the case here. 8 April 2009.

No. 66598 is passing Stapleford and Sandiacre shunt frame box with 6L45 07.37 Earles–West Thurrock loaded cement, the impressive box having around four months left in use at this point before being made redundant by the Erewash Valley resignalling. 2 June 2009.

Nos 60024 and 66187 cross the ladder at Stapleford and Sandiacre with a mixed consist 6M73 10.52 Doncaster Decoy–Toton North yard, passing the now empty shell of the shunt frame box, which lingered on until being demolished two months after this image was taken. This shot was taken exactly two years to the day after the pic of No. 66726. 8 April 2011.

Ten years on from the shot of No. 66726, yard pilot No. 60074 is propelling a rake of Coalfish wagons into Stapleford and Sandiacre sidings as No. 66603 approaches with 6G65 09.14 Earles–Walsall cement. The last remnants of the foot crossing are all that remain to remind that the shunt frame box used to stand here. 13 May 2019.

Yard pilot No. 08441 is shunting a rake of MGR hoppers in Old Bank yard. Note the crude painting out of the BR double arrow symbol on the bodyside. 3 June 1996.

On a bitterly cold December morning, No. 58035 catches the early morning glint of the low sun as it arrives at Toton with 7H95 08.26 Calverton colliery–Ratcliffe power station, which will back onto New Bank yard before running round to await its departure slot to the power station. 3 December 1997.

No. 37899 is acting as yard pilot, substituting for a Class 08 and is seen shunting a rake of Seacow wagons into Stapleford and Sandicare ballast sidings. 13 August 1998.

No. 60036 passes through Toton with 6E88 15.27 Corby steelworks–Lackenby empty coils, as an MGR departs south from the Old Bank and two Class 58s sit on empty MGR sets in the North yard. 6 May 1999.

No. 56049, in Dutch-Transrail livery, backs 6G44 12.46 Bescot Yard–Toton into Old Bank Yard. The train is a 'Slinger' train conveying long welded rails. The arms on the wagons act like cranes to lift the rails and deliver them over the side of the wagons. 1 May 2002.

No. 08511 is shunting a rake of Railtrack PNA wagons in New Bank, the shunt loco looking resplendent in newly applied EWS colours. Prior to being painted, the loco had been operating for some while in red oxide primer, with the unofficial name *James* on the battery box. 1 May 2002.

Southern Region Electro-Diesels were once very rarely seen away from their home territory, unlike current times with the type seen as far north as Inverness and Fort William. Therefore in 2001, when I was told that No. 73131 was going to work a 6Z11 15.50 Leicester LIP–Toton with the depot fuel tanks, it was a huge working. The loco was being moved to Toton for its paintwork to be tidied in readiness for a forthcoming Royal train working, and is seen here propelling the tanks into New Bank sidings. 7 March 2001.

No. 60019 *PATHFINDER TOURS 30 YEARS OF RAILTOURING 1973–2003* in the original EW&S livery is seen moving two rail-mounted cranes from Toton North yard to Sandiacre ballast sidings, passing the shed with more than forty classmates on view, many of which will likely never run again. No. 60019 itself was officially stored when this photo was taken, but subsequently received a Super-Sixty overhaul by DB Schenker at Toton, and was repainted into DB red livery. 2 June 2009.

Class 20 Nos 20142 and 20189 are no strangers to Toton, but not in this livery. Gleaming in freshly applied Balfour Beatty Rail colours, they are seen propelling two FKA flats into the Balfour Beatty yard at Sandiacre having just arrived as 6Z41 from Doncaster West yard. The locos wore this livery for a very short period before they were repainted again. 6 May 2014.

No. 67024 tails 1O07 17.21 Chesterfield–London Victoria VSOE Pullman through Toton, taking day trippers that have been to visit the Chatsworth estate back to the capital. 9 July 2014.

WCRC's No. 47245 tops-and-tails with No. 47851 passing the shed with 1Z47 06.12 Leicester–Carlisle charter, which would later enjoy steam traction as part of its itinerary. The shed has plenty of traction on view, including two Colas-liveried Class 60s. 2 July 2016.

Toton New Bank yard was returning to nature as seen in this view from the A52 bridge with thirty stored and withdrawn Class 60s on view bringing some colour to the otherwise mostly green scene. The yard was deforested in 2021 amid rumours of reuse now that HS2 will no longer use the land, but at the time of writing this has not yet taken place. 12 August 2019.

HS2 PLANS WITHDRAWN. *See 208*
21/11/2021 D. RadPart 28/12/2022

DC Rail Freight Nos 56103 and 56091 *Driver Wayne Gaskell – The Godfather* power through Toton on the Down Erewash fast line with 6Z55 16.40 Derby Chaddesden yard–Carlisle Kingmoor yard. The greenery between Old and New Bank yards had really taken hold and was obscuring some of the stored Class 60s. 12 August 2019.

A new service that started running on the Erewash in 2019 was the 'Tesco Express' from Tees Dock to Daventry and return. On a Sunday it returned north in the evening, giving a chance to capture the train as it was nicely lit from the A52. Here No. 66303 is getting away from its booked crew stop, working as 4E49 16.09 Daventry–South Bank Tees Dock. 24 May 2020.

After passing under the A52 bridge at Stapleford and Sandiacre, No. 44009 is seen with a short engineers train that is coming to a stand after arriving from the south. The train will then propel into Stapleford and Sandiacre ballast sidings. No. 44009 was the only Class 44 to receive a headcode panel after accident damage was repaired. 24 September 1978. (J. Freebury)

Former Burry Port and Gwendraeth cut down cab loco No. 08993 *ASHBURNHAM* spent a period working as a pilot loco based at Toton. On this day the loco was captured transferring a Salmon wagon from the Old Bank to the North yard. 23 September 1998.

In the early 1990s it was the turn of the EE Type 1 Class 20 locos to be phased out with large numbers of the class laid up around the Toton site, and also at Stanton Gate. Here two lines of locos were stored in the sidings adjacent to the main entrance and former Rugby Portland cement buildings. With no security gate in those days, they were prime targets for vandals and thieves. In this view Nos 20058, 20148, 20170, 20197, 20010, 20141, 20028 and 20074 are visible. 11 September 1992.

No. 37055 *RAIL Celebrity* approaches Toton with 8X10 09.25 Horbury Prorail–Didcot yard, conveying an overhauled set of 1973 Piccadilly line stock that would be tripped forward from Didcot to West Ruislip the following morning. This was my third shot of the train at different spots, after it was stopped for a period at the signal just north of the road bridge – and all chasing was by push bike! 4 June 1997.

Class 20s No. 8023 in green livery and No. 20228 in BR blue approach Toton from the Stanton Gate direction with a coal train *c.* spring 1974. Note the large Stanton ironworks on the horizon, which provided much freight activity in the local area with raw products taken in and finished products out. (PR Collection)

Brush Type 4 No. 47515 rushes through Stapleford and Sandiacre with the 'Master Cutler' 16.55 St Pancras–Sheffield, passing the Rugby Portland cement company terminal. 21 July 1982. (P. Kazmierczak)

No. 45001 arrives at Stapleford and Sandiacre with 4 TTA oil tanks from Colwick. The train will stop behind the semaphore disc. Once the route is set and the signal cleared, it will set back into the Old Bank. 20 September 1984. (C. Smith)

Railfreight red stripe No. 20215 and BR blue No. 20142 are seen setting back into New Bank yard with MGR empties from Ratcliffe power station. 14 June 1991. (PR Collection)

No. 58050 *Toton Traction Depot* stands at Stapleford and Sandiacre waiting to be accepted into Toton yard, with 6B08 07.59 Kirkby in Ashfield–Toton Old Bank engineering train. Alongside the train, the Down goods line is under an engineers possession with a steel sleeper relay in progress. 30 July 2000.

St Giles' church in Sandiacre dominates the background as Class 47 No. 47016 *ATLAS* (missing its nameplate on this side) approaches Toton with 7M63 08.19 Doncaster Wood yard–Mountsorrel ballast empties. 5 September 1997.

Single Class 20 No. 20134 stands at the signal on the Up goods at Stapleford and Sandiacre with a mixed freight, awaiting acceptance into Toton Old Bank. The Old Cross Dyeworks Ltd factory provides the industrial backdrop. 28 April 1978. (J. Woolley)

No. 66721 *Harry Beck*, in London Transport map livery, arrives at Toton with 6M73 10.52 from Doncaster Decoy yard conveying spoil empties and flats loaded with concrete sleepers. The location has seen changes to the infrastructure with Toton North Junction now at this spot, and the surroundings have changed greatly with the dyeworks consigned to history. 2 March 2017.